ROSINA SEDIBANE MODIBA

A DREAM DENIED

LORATO TROK

dp davidphilip

Second edition 2021 published by
David Philip Publishers trading as New Africa Books
Unit 13, Athlone Industrial Park
10 Mymoena Crescent
Athlone Industrial Park
7764
Cape Town
South Africa

First edition published 2019 by Geko Publishing, *Against the Odds*

ISBN: 978-1-4856-3055-5
eBook ISBN: 978-1-4856-3056-2

Editing: Nicola Rijsdijk
Proofreading: Melissa Fagan
Layout and design: Peter Stuckey and Rupert Pluck
Cover design: Rupert Pluck

Photographic Credits: Every effort has been made to trace and
acknowledge copyright holders. Where we have not been successful, we
will be pleased to rectify any omissions at the earliest opportunity.

Printing and binding: Novus Print

*David Philip is committed to a sustainable future for our business, our readers,
our country, and the world.*

Contents

Dedication

To all the unsung heroes and heroines

Foreword

I first met Lorato Trok in the closing decade of the 20th century. That is how long we have known each other! At the time I was on the Advisory Board of the Centre for the Book, where Lorato was a member of staff. One of her responsibilities was running First Words in Print, a project that was started on the principle that the first words a child sees in print should reflect their own language and environment. This was one of my favourite projects because it resonated with my view that education should move from the particular to the universal and not the other way around.

Those of us who grew up in a colonial system were taught the language and history of our colonisers, while the knowledge within our own communities was not considered worthy of serious academic enquiry. We grew up reading children's literature that reflected a white Western world and we did not see ourselves in this literature. That is why the reclaiming of our own stories should be at the heart of the decolonisation project.

Books should act as both mirrors and windows – mirrors in which children can see and know themselves, and windows through which they learn about the rest of the world beyond their immediate environment. This has been the principle underlying Lorato Trok's work. Lorato and Elizabeth Anderson, the Head of Centre for the Book, worked very hard with publishers to produce the First Words in Print series, a beautiful set of proudly South African books for early childhood. Lorato's commitment to producing quality multilingual children's literature continued through her work at Room to Read, the African Storybook Project and finally the Puku Children's Literature Foundation, where I have had the pleasure of working with her as a valued colleague.

I was extremely excited when Lorato shared the Rosina Modiba manuscript with me. It resonated with our shared passion about developing an indigenous children's literature. It also spoke to my love for athletics and my long-held view that Africans have dominated the world athletics stage and yet there are few books about African runners. I once worked with friends in Ethiopia on a children's book about legendary Ethiopian runner Haile Gebrselassie. Sadly, that book did not reach publication stage and this book on Rosina Modiba has encouraged me to go back to the drawing board and complete the Haile project.

If the Rosina story could inspire me, I am sure that it can inspire young people to pursue their athletic dreams, even in the face of the many hurdles that confront them. Hopefully it will inspire our education and sports institutions to uncover the stories of many of our unsung heroes who struggled against almost insurmountable hurdles to make their mark in the country's sporting history.

I am so glad that Rosina Modiba was generous enough to share her story and that Lorato Trok was disciplined enough to write it. I sincerely hope that as many young people as possible will have access to the book and will take the time to read it.

Elinor Sisulu

Preface

I grew up in a small town in the Northern Cape in the late 1980s and early 1990s, far from the hustle and bustle of big cities like Johannesburg and Pretoria. But even there, everyone knew the story of Zola Budd, a white athlete who was considered a running sensation in South Africa and across the globe. Zola Budd was really popular. In the townships, there were minibus taxis named "Zola Budd", largely for their speed. Brenda Fassie, the "Queen of African Pop", dubbed the "Madonna of the Townships" by *Time* magazine, penned a song called "Zola Budd" about a minibus taxi. The song became a popular township anthem in the 1990s. That Zola Budd could be that celebrated in townships battered by policies of white minority rule during the dark days of apartheid speaks to how stories of black women get lost while privileging the achievements of white women.

I first learnt of Rosina Sedibane Modiba in 2013, when an organisation I was working for piloted a digital-publishing platform for children's literature in a few schools in Atteridgeville. So little has been written about her that I had gone through all my years of schooling without any knowledge of

Rosina's achievements as a track and field star in the 1970s. Rosina's story has been invisible in South Africa, and even people who grew up in and around **Tshwane** have never heard her name. Chrystal Nkwana is one such person.

In 2002, Chrystal Nkwana was a few months into her position as principal of Bathokwa Primary School in Saulsville. Along with a number of other principals from schools around Tshwane, she was invited to the opening of Rosina Sedibane Modiba Sport School of Focused Learning in Laudium. She did not think anything of it – it was just one of the perks of her position. She was oblivious both to who this Rosina Sedibane was, and to the achievements that had led to her having a school named after her.

At the ceremony, Chrystal heard whispers around her. It was unfair, people were saying, that Rosina was absent from the ceremony while her principal was there. It was only when another school's principal confronted her that Chrystal realised they were talking about *her* school. *She* was the principal everyone was talking about! When Chrystal explained that she had no idea who Rosina was, she was informed that a teacher named Rosina Modiba at her school was the same Rosina Sedibane that the new school had been named after. When the invitation had arrived at her school's office, it had born Rosina's maiden surname, Sedibane. Chrystal had only just met Rosina and knew nothing about her past sporting achievements.

It was a shock to Chrystal that there was no literature available on Rosina and her achievements. Chrystal could not believe that one of her teachers was an unsung heroine, one whom fellow teachers and children at her school knew nothing about.

Today, Chrystal ensures that visitors to Bathokwa Primary School leave the school fully aware of Rosina's athletic prowess. She makes sure that Rosina tells her story to the children of Bathokwa at the beginning of each school year.

In recent years, Rosina has been invited by government departments, the private sector and civil society organisations to appear at their events. Even so, Chrystal believes that Rosina's sporting achievements have not been acknowledged enough, for which she blames gender bias in South African sports. "Rosina should not only be invited to sports events," Chrystal says. "She should be recognised in a way that speaks to her achievements."

Black women's contributions to society have been left out of history books the world over – their achievements have either been whitewashed or falsely credited to other people. Rosina's name has been used to name a school, but her story has never been told. She is a South African heroine who paved the way for a generation of the country's athletes. athletes. Until her retirement, she continued to contribute as a primary-school teacher in her home town of Atteridgeville, Tshwane.

The story of Rosina Sedibane Modiba is one of resilience in the face of an inhumane system of racial discrimination. It is a story of rebellion against cultural traditions and norms dictated by a patriarchal society that devalues black women.

This book is a celebration of Rosina's tenacity and the role she played in changing the course of history – against all odds. From birth to adulthood, Rosina's life story reads like it was written in the stars.

Lorato Trok

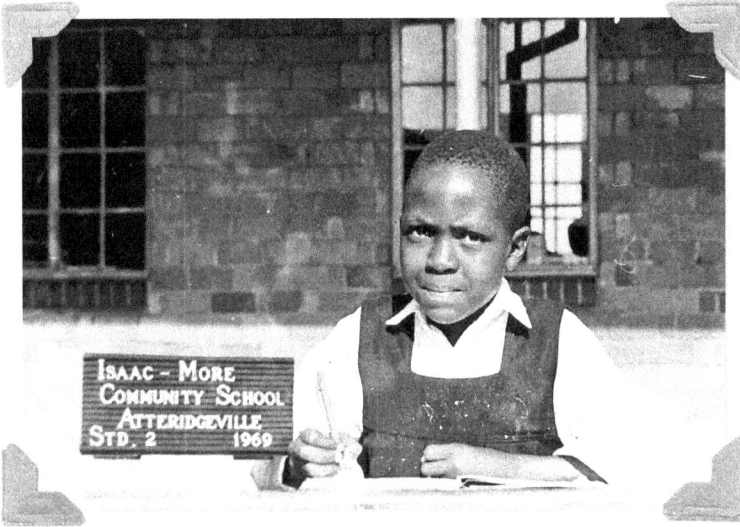

Rosina as a schoolgirl in 1969, aged 10

CHAPTER 1

Off the starting block

For a black child born in **apartheid** South Africa in the late 1950s, life was never going to be easy. In many ways, the laws of the country were designed to stand in the way of individual success.

This was the South Africa that Rosina Sedibane was born into on the morning of 26 December 1958. The Sedibanes had been expecting the arrival of their fourth child the day before, because their eldest daughter, Margaret, had also been born on Christmas Day. But baby Rosina forged her own path and arrived a day later.

> Masegou Martha Sedibane and Mothabi Johannes Sedibane were liberal parents who let their children choose their own paths in life, and their family was close-knit and happy.

Rosina's parents, Masegou Martha Sedibane and Mothabi Johannes Sedibane, had settled in Laudium just outside Pretoria (today's Tshwane) in the 1950s, having moved from Ga-Phaahla village in the then Lebowakgomo **Bantustan** (today's Limpopo Province). They were liberal parents who let their children choose their own paths in life, and their family was close-knit and happy.

Because she had beaten the odds, the nurses nicknamed her "Mosadi", a Setswana name for "woman".

After Rosina's birth, Masegou fell sick, leaving the doctors and nurses unable to diagnose her mysterious condition. Newborn Rosina was left in the care of the nurses and her father was told that the baby was unlikely to survive her first days without her mother. But as the days went by, baby Rosina grew healthy and strong. Because she had beaten the odds, the nurses nicknamed her "**Mosadi**", a Setswana name for "woman".

After a few months, Masegou and baby Rosina were discharged from hospital, but another hurdle awaited them at home. The apartheid government had cracked down on multiracial communities by enforcing the **Group Areas Act**, which legislated residential segregation throughout the country. African, coloured and Indian families were being forcibly removed from land earmarked for whites, and relocated to distant townships. The Sedibanes were not spared this trauma: when Laudium was prescribed an Indian settlement, they were moved to Atteridgeville, a township west of Pretoria.

Having returned home from hospital, Masegou was still not well enough to take care of her new baby, so she moved to her parents in Ga-Phaahla to recuperate, taking Rosina with her. It was only four years later, in 1962, that little Rosina and her mother, now stronger and healthier, rejoined the rest of the family in Atteridgeville.

While Rosina had been called "Mosadi" in hospital, as she grew she became known as "**Mosetsana**", the girl child, a name her peers would later change to "The Girl". It was this name that she would adopt as her running name and it would stick with her always.

◇◇◇

Masegou had never gone to school, because as soon as she was deemed fit and grown-up enough, she was set to herding cattle.

When Rosina was a little girl, her mother sometimes told her how difficult it had been growing up in rural Lebowakgomo. Masegou had never gone to school, because as soon as she was deemed fit and grown-up enough, she was set to herding cattle. She told her daughters that as a young girl, she had been able to outrun all her fellow herders, including the boys, when they were chasing cows in the village, and she used to beat her peers at games like **diketo** and **morabaraba**. Rosina also heard stories about her father, Johannes. He told her how as a young boy in rural Lebowa he had been able to outrun rabbits and catch them with his own hands.

It would seem that the young Rosina would follow in her parents' footsteps – there was never a time when running was not a part of her life. Rosina ran everywhere. When she was sent to the shops, it seemed to everyone that she would arrive as soon as she had left, having run there and back at lightning speed. In Atteridgeville she soon became a poster child for obedience: if other children loafed around when they were supposed to be on errands, their parents would remind them how quickly Rosina would have done the task.

At the age of seven, in her first year at Isaac More Primary School in Attridgeville, Rosina ran for the

> Athletics was not considered a female sport in her community, and the teachers focused mostly on training and developing boys.

school as a reserve. This meant that she never won races, but was seen as being good enough to replace the best runners when the need arose. At primary school, children did not race by age but by height. Rosina was taller than most children her age, and was thus always paired with older children. By the time she moved to Patogeng Higher Primary School, Rosina was winning races against children who were older than her.

Rosina loved to run, but no one paid much attention. Athletics was not considered a female sport in her community, and the teachers focused mostly on training and developing boys. As a girl, she felt like an afterthought, but she continued to follow her passion.

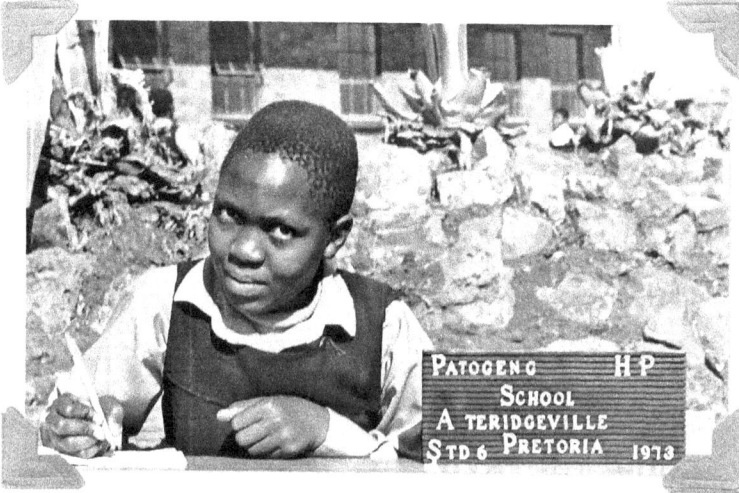

Rosina as a schoolgirl in 1973, aged 14

CHAPTER 2

Schoolgirl sensation

In 1973, at fourteen years old, Rosina won the 800 metres in the junior section of the inter-high schools championships.

Rosina at the 1975
inter-high schools championships

The championships were a display of the cream of the crop in black high schools across the country, and Rosina's win was a sign of things to come.

In 1974, Rosina started at Hofmeyr High School, and it was there that her athletics ability was finally nurtured. At Hofmeyr, the requirement was that athletes could only participate in two races, but they competed in age groups rather than by height, and the teachers chose athletes based on their strengths and what sporting codes they excelled in.

Rosina with her sister Margaret at their home in Atteridgeville after receiving miniature trophies from the inter-high schools championships, 1975

By then it had become obvious that Rosina was strong in 1 500- and 800-metre races. She was just as good in long jump, and in the 400 and 3 000 metres. With the opportunity to compete, Rosina began to blossom.

◇◇◇

It was around this time that Rosina crossed paths with James Mokoka, a sports administrator who was scouting for sporting talent in black high schools. Mokoka had already formed the **Soweto** Hartze, South Africa's first black athletics club, and the Atteridgeville Athletics Club. He would later establish the first black athletics clubs in the Pretoria townships of Soshanguve, Atteridgeville, Garankuwa and Mabopane – the latter is still active.

Mokoka made it his mission to identify black female athletes, focusing on Atteridgeville's well-known Hofmeyr High School, which was known for sporting excellence and commitment.

Mokoka knew that black female athletes were few and far between and underrepresented in some athletics codes, and this was a concern for him. He made it his mission to identify black female athletes, focusing on Atteridgeville's well-known Hofmeyr High School, which was known for sporting excellence and commitment. He was looking to identify promising sprinters when he noticed the impressive performances of Rosina, her sister Margaret and some other schoolgirl athletes.

Some of the "Dream Team" — from the back left, Margaret Sedibane, Mamiki, Foroza Shaka and Kholofelo Dlamini; at the front are Rosina and another runner called Margaret

Coach James Mokoka and athletes Rosina Sedibane, George Mosoeu and Sydney Maree

CHAPTER 3

A world-class coach

James Mokoka's motto for his athletes was: "bloed, sweat and trane" (blood, sweat and tears). Whether in the pouring rain or the blistering heat of the **Northern Transvaal**, his athletes knew that they were expected to answer the call of duty.

> ## Mokoka was used to traditionalist parents and a deeply patriarchal community that considered the idea of female athletes taboo.

Mokoka was a no-nonsense coach who expected commitment from his athletes. He was known for his discipline and world-class administrative abilities.

Coach Mokoka set his sights on a number of girls who he believed had great potential and who varied in talent ranging from sprinters to hurdlers, and from middle-distance to cross-country runners. But first he had to convince their parents to let them run. Mokoka was used to traditionalist parents and a deeply patriarchal community that considered the idea of female athletes taboo. Some parents were supportive of James, however, and gave him permission to coach their daughters. He was pleased that the Sedibanes easily agreed to let their girl children partake in running.

Although he started with a good number of girls, some fell by the wayside. Those who stayed the course would become his most prized team, known in the township as the "Dream Team". It was made up of Linda Shabangu in hurdles, Junia Motau, Alice Malokane, Pharees Masekwameng, Pretty Mohokane and the Sedibane siblings, Rosina and Margaret, as sprinters.

In a patriarchal society, Coach Mokoka had to work hard to instill a sense of self-love in the girls.

But things were not easy. Coach Mokoka had no sponsorship for his team and his athletes lacked exposure and therefore struggled with low self-esteem. He remembers a time when he managed to get a sponsorship of tracksuits for his female team. It was a struggle to get the girls to wear the tracksuits from their homes to the stadium: "They did not think that they deserved new kits and they were struggling with the thought of being seen by people in the township with pants on," remembers Coach Mokoka. In a patriarchal society, he had to work hard to instill a sense of self-love in the girls.

Coach Mokoka's training tactics could be considered unorthodox, but his methods worked for him and his athletes. Once, he dropped off Rosina and the other team members on the main road in Atteridgeville and instructed them to run all the way to the Atteridgeville Super Stadium (now Lucas Masterpieces Moripe Stadium) on the other end of the township.

"At one stage, my 16-year-old body could not take it any longer and I broke down," Rosina remembers. "Coach Mokoka asked me if I wanted to stop, but I refused and kept running, with tears running down my face. He always reminded us that coaching us was our story and not his."

Through his job as a sports administrator for the city council, Coach Mokoka frequently travelled outside of Pretoria to train other sports coaches, and he had his female team travel with him so that he could continue training them. He took them everywhere, and would make arrangements for them to continue their studies at schools in areas where he was working. All his athletes had different training schedules because they were all running different disciplines.

◇◇◇

Coach Mokoka had a much bigger vision for his team than anyone realised. His team became the cream of the crop in the township and across black South Africa. Kenneth Lebethe, acclaimed black reporter for the *Pretoria News*, took it upon himself to promote black athletes, particularly Coach Mokoka's "Dream Team". Kenneth and the legendary John Malapane, host on Radio Lebowa (now Thobela FM) became the voices of the voiceless in the townships.

Coach Mokoka had a much bigger vision for his team than anyone realised. His team became the cream of the crop in the township and across black South Africa.

Sydney Maree, who found fame in the international arena in the 1980s after his move to the US, had this to say in January 2018:

All of us wouldn't be where we are without Ntate Mokoka. He

had a mission. He identified
the mission, and he had decided
that at whatever cost he would
undertake the mission. At the
time it was extremely difficult
for black women through
the system of apartheid and a
patriarchal society. He was a
disciplinarian and an impeccable
administrator. He should be one
of the highest-ranking sports
administrators in the country
today, training and developing
athletes and administrators.

The lonely Rose

A girl who will go a long way — and do it in record time

Supplement to the Rand Daily Mail,
January 31, 1979

CHAPTER 4

A one-woman show

Young Rosina was now an 800-,
1 500-, 3 000-metre and
cross-country athlete.

She was dedicated and improved her running time whenever she raced. Rosina always remembered Coach Mokoka's encouraging words that they were only running against their own time, and she lived by them.

Rosina had already developed a reputation for her athletic prowess. Unbeknownst to her, the other athletes had rejoiced that she was late, and many had hoped that she would miss the competition altogether.

The South African Schools (Black) Championships were held annually in winter in Welkom in what was then the Orange Free State (now the Free State). In anticipation of the 1974 event, the girls were joined by Sydney Maree, the first male athlete to join Coach Mokoka's all-female team.

To partake in the competition, Rosina and Sydney were to travel from Pretoria to Welkom by train. Along the way, the train broke down, and it ended up taking them a full day to reach Welkom. By then, Rosina had already developed a reputation for her athletic prowess. Unbeknownst to her, the other athletes had rejoiced that she was late, and many had hoped that she would miss the competition altogether.

When she and Sydney entered the stadium, it reverberated with applause from the excited spectators, but there was disappointment in the eyes of their

Fifteen-year-old Rosina broke the 800m record at the SA Schools Championships in Welkom, 1974 (seen here in the supplement to the Rand Daily Mail, 31 January 1979)

> Rosina's teammates pleaded with her to not embarrass them by opening wide spaces.

competitors. One of the athletes became visibly upset and told Rosina that she wished she had never arrived. Rosina's teammates pleaded with her to not embarrass them by opening wide spaces. Both Sydney and Rosina went on to win their respective races. In the 800 and 1 500 metres, it wouldn't be a stretch to call it a one-woman show – Rosina was streets ahead of her teammates with the second-place runner trailing some ten metres behind her.

> Dominating every race she entered, and even breaking her own records, she was becoming the best-known young track star, first in Atteridgeville and then in all of Pretoria.

As the schools athletics season was closing, Coach Mokoka's "Dream Team" continued to train. For more rigorous exercise, Coach Mokoka used the training grounds at the mines. Being the first and only female team there, they had to compete against themselves, and against the male running club Coach Mokoka had formed years earlier in Soweto.

Rosina continued to excel in the 800- and 1 500-metre races, beating both her own teammates and the Soweto team. Dominating every race she entered, and even breaking her own records, she was becoming the best-known young track star, first in Atteridgeville and then in all of Pretoria.

At fifteen, Rosina was an athletic marvel.

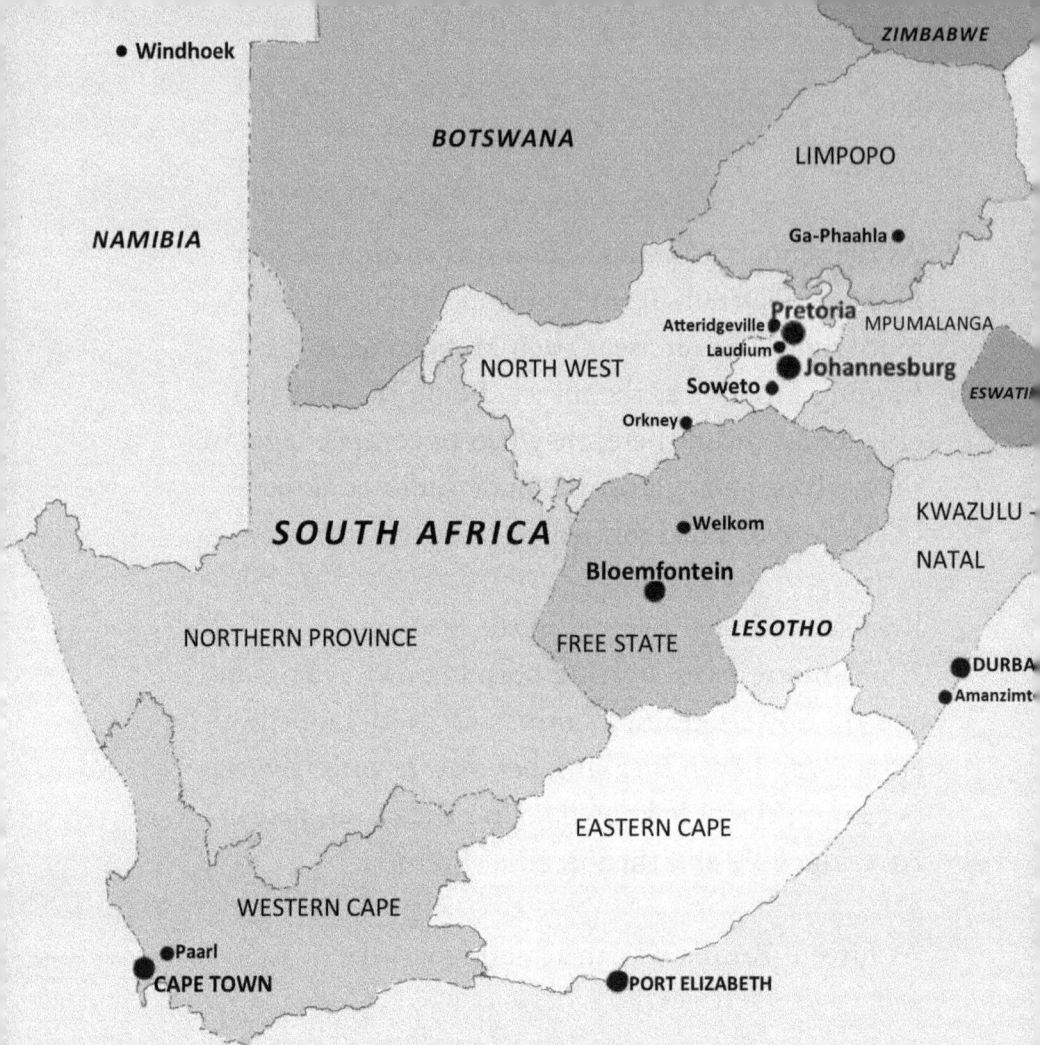

ZIMBABWE

• Windhoek

BOTSWANA

LIMPOPO

NAMIBIA

Ga-Phaahla •

Pretoria
Atteridgeville •
Laudium •   MPUMALANGA
NORTH WEST   • Johannesburg
Soweto •

ESWATI

Orkney •

SOUTH AFRICA   • Welkom

KWAZULU -
NATAL

Bloemfontein

• DURBA

NORTHERN PROVINCE   FREE STATE   LESOTHO

Amanzimt

EASTERN CAPE

WESTERN CAPE

• Paarl
CAPE TOWN   PORT ELIZABETH

© Nicolaas Maritz September

Port Elizabeth Chevrolet Invitation 1976
From left to right: Cheryl Primmer,
Aneen de Jager and Rosina Sedibane

CHAPTER 5

Making history

Black female athletes in the 1970s
did not have organised sporting codes,
and things were even more difficult
in athletics.

Athletics as a sport for black women was underdeveloped and of a much lower standard than that of their white counterparts.

Coach Mokoka was met with a sceptical public who had little confidence in the abilities of the female athlete in his club. Black male athletes had become organised and had years of experience as they belonged to the better-resourced running clubs owned by the mines, and white athletes had structures available through favourable apartheid laws. Athletics as a sport for black women was underdeveloped and of a much lower standard than that of their white counterparts.

Added to that, black athletes were only allowed to compete against white athletes by invitation, when their performance was deemed worthy and at the discretion of the white sports administrators. Coach Mokoka had to send his athletes' running times for assessment after each competitive race they ran in the black federation. This was a deliberate tactic by the apartheid government, which was careful in the process of selecting races in which black athletes could participate. Rosina and her sister Margaret Sedibane were two of the few black athletes invited to compete at the multicultural races.

With the lack of resources in the townships, Coach Mokoka faced insurmountable challenges. Some female athletes only joined his team because they saw the athletes wearing new tracksuits, and many struggled with the rigorous training schedule and the pressure of patriarchy and tradition. Coach Mokoka had started with a good number of girls, but some soon fell by the wayside. Those like Rosina who stayed the course faced discrimination from all angles, and many a time Coach Mokoka had to act as psychologist to boost the team's confidence. With the odds stacked against them, it was difficult to keep the female team going.

◊◊◊

In 1975, Rosina made history when she became the first black woman from the South African Amateur Athletic Union (SAAAU) to feature in the mixed-race South African Multinational Cross Country Championship. The only other black athletes were from neighbouring countries like Rhodesia (now

For the first time, black women athletes took part in the SA Cross-Country Championships at Maraisburg. From left to right: Busi Chuma (Rhodesia), Lois Abel (Rhodesia), R Makhaye (Rhodesia), Siphiwe Mandishona (Rhodesia), D Mkhaze, Rosina Sedibane, M Moloi (South Africa), Jean Lockhead (Great Britain) and Annette Welgemoed (South Africa)

Zimbabwe) – besides them, the only other black people at the stadium were the coaches and the technical team. With the handful of black people seated in the less desirable section of the stadium, Rosina was confronted, for the first time in her life, with a sea of white faces.

"I remember being extremely nervous, shaking with fear not knowing how to handle being around white people," Rosina said in an interview many years later.

"Their hostility towards the black athletes did not help."

"Coach Mokoka had organised an Adidas running outfit for me, from running shorts to running shoes, but it was not as fancy as the other athletes'," she remembers.

He told her that she might not have the advantage of resources similar to her competitors, but that they had one thing in common: their legs. She did not win this race, coming in at twenty-two, but the experience gave her renewed confidence. Inspired by Coach Makoka's formidable coaching style, Rosina developed an inner determination.

Later that year, at the age of only sixteen, Rosina Sedibane became the first black South African woman to win the 1 500 middle-distance race against white South African women athletes. By this time she already held records for the 400, 600, 800, 1 500 and 3 000 races in the then confederation for black athletes, the South African Amateur Athletics and Cycling Federation (SAAA&CF). Although she had no sponsorship, Rosina would go on to win many races against white athletes and shame the apartheid government.

Aneen de Jager and
Rosina chat after the race

Rosina came second in the 800m at the
Vernon Barnes Memorial Meeting 1976, after
Aneen de Jager (pictured second to the left)

CHAPTER 6

Rising up

As a teenager, Rosina had a very definite
passion for athletics: she just wanted
to run, and she continued to train hard
under the guidance of Coach Mokoka.

But politics was never far from the lives of all young people in the townships; it affected every facet of their days.

The year 1976 would be a turning point for the seventeen-year-old Rosina, as it was for many young black people in South Africa. The country was gripped by political violence that would soon lead to the **Soweto uprising**, and Rosina would be caught in the crossfire. On 16 June 1976, black schoolchildren rose up against apartheid's unjust laws. The demonstration started in Soweto, but soon spread to other townships – including Atteridgeville.

Politics was never far from the lives of all young people in the townships; it affected every facet of their days.

Rosina remembers how she took to the streets along with her peers. "There was a huge sense of fearlessness in all of us, including children as young as seven years old from primary school," she remembers.

After confronting the police, the crowd Rosina had joined was forced to disperse. As she was running away, a bullet grazed her head. Rosina did not suffer any real injuries, but her hair never grew on that part of her head again.

Following the Soweto uprising, the atmosphere in the townships was so politically charged that Hofmeyr High School in Atteridgeville completely shut down for the rest of the year, and students were unable to sit for their final exams. Rosina and most of her peers had to repeat a grade in 1977, but for the class of 1976, it was worth the sacrifice.

Rose Sedibane, knap jong swart atleet van Transvaal, wat Woensdagaand in die U.P.E.-stadion by die 13de Chevrolet Vernon Barnes- gedenkbyeenkoms die eerste swart vrou sal wees om in dié stadion te hardloop. Hier wen sy die 800 vir meisies o.18 op die De Loorskild-byeenkoms. Sy is die eerste swart vrou wat 'n veelrassige wedloop in Suid-Afrika gewen het. Rose vlieg Woensdag na Port Elizabeth saam met Sydney Maree en hul bekende afrigter James Makoka, wat vir die Sportstigting werk.

Prior to the Vernon Barnes Memorial, this newspaper caption from 13 December 1976 introduces Rosina as the first black woman to run in the UPE stadium, and also notes that she was the first black woman in South Africa to win a mixed-race athletics event.

The events of that year were to have a profound effect on the lives of a whole generation of South Africans. But while the voices of the youth had been heard in all corners of the country, political change was slow. In athletics as well as in other spheres of South African life, ordinary people continued to come up against apartheid's crushing laws.

> ## The events of that year were to have a profound effect on the lives of a whole generation of South Africans.

The events of that year were to have a profound effect on the lives of a whole generation of South Africans.

◇◇◇

But Rosina was destined for more success. In 1976 she broke a 1 500-metre record at Vaal Reefs Mine in Orkney, becoming the first black woman athlete to win a gold medal over that distance.

On 15 December of the same year, Rosina and Sydney Maree were the only black athletes to be invited to the Vernon Barnes Memorial meeting in Port Elizabeth. Rosina remembers the events of the day vividly. She recalls that the atmosphere was

On 15 December of the same year, Rosina and Sydney Maree were the only black athletes to be invited to the Vernon Barnes Memorial meeting in Port Elizabeth.

abuzz with talk of a new hero: in the one-mile race, Sydney Maree had succeeded in an iconic win against crowd favourite, Clive Dale.

Rosina went on to become the second big surprise at this middle-distance meeting by beating established athletes and finishing second in the 800 metres behind South African (white federation) record-holder, Aneen de Jager.

ROSE SIDIBANE, the leading Black woman middle-distance runner in South Africa, who is flying from Pretoria today to compete in the 800 metres at the Vernon Barnes memorial meeting at UPE tonight.

Rosina pictured in The Herald in anticipation of her 800m race at the Vernon Barnes Memorial meeting, 1976

YDNEY MAREE is not the only black student to make history — 16 year-old Rosie Sedibane, also of Pretoria, has become the first Black girl to reach the top flight of athletics in South Africa.

At the Vernon Barnes meeting in 1976, Sydney Maree broke the one-mile record. He is the first black person to come in under 4 minutes (at a time of 3:53.7) - the fourth fastest mile ever achieved by a South African.

Rosina also set a new record of 2 minutes, 9.5 seconds in the 800 metres in the SAAAU (black federation), as well as records in the 400 and 3 000 metres.

On 26 December 1976, two weeks after finishing second to Aneen de Jager, Rosina was invited to participate at the annual Paarl Boxing Day games. She remembers the raucous crowds when she beat Eloise Steyn and Marieta Nel to claim the top spot in the 800-metre race.

Rosina had spent Christmas Day travelling to Paarl for this competition. The win meant so much to her, not only because it made up for not being able to spend Christmas with her family but because it took place on her milestone eighteenth birthday.

It was just six months after the 1976 uprisings, when Rosina had outrun a bullet to save her life. Now she was racing for glory.

Atletiek in die Paarl

Die uitslae van gister se atletiek by die Gesinsdag byeenkoms in die Paarl is: *(Burger 28/12/76)*

MANS

100: 1. J. Carlos (VSA) 10,8; 2. J. Bezuidenhout (Tyg) 11,0; 3. B. Voss (P-O) 11,2.
200: 1. J. Carlos (VSA) 21,8; 2. J. Bezuidenhout (Tyg) 22,7; 3. B. Voss (P-O) 23,0.
400: 1. C. Nel (UK) 49,9; 2. F. Lombard (Bell) 50,0; 3. K. Dyamond (CH) 50,1.
800: 1. S. Maree (Pret) 1:49,9; 2. J. du Plessis (US) 1:52,1; 3. C. Farrel (Pinelands) 1:54,4.
1 myl: 1. S. Maree (Pret) 4:08,8; 2. T. Marsay (RAU) 4:10,9; 3. P. Joseph (P-O) 4:22,2.
5 000: 1. E. Bonzet (SH) 14:44,6; 2. T. Marsay (RAU) 3. M. Bosch (UPE).
3 000 h: 1. J. Siebrits (US) 9:08,4; 2. D. Cronje (UPE); 3. P. Joseph (P-O).
110 h: 1. T. Galloway (Bell) 14,9; 2. A. Lategan (US) 15,0; 3. B. Farrell (UK) 15,1.
400 h: 1. T. Galloway (Bell) 53,8; 2. D. v.d. Merwe (RAU) 53,9; 3. J. Bouwer (US) 56,5.
5 000 stap: 1. T. Kluyts (US) 24:04,0; 2. N. Kluyts (US) 26:01,6; 3. J. de Jager (Adamantia) 26:05,0.
HS: 1. J. Wolhuter (US) 1,95; 2. D. Wolhuter (De Kullen) 1,83; 3. J. McLachlan (Bell) 1,78.
VS: 1. J. v.d. Merwe (ST) 6,75; 2. T. Galloway (Bell) 6,55; 3. A. v.d. Burg (UP) 6,14.
PS: 1. A. Franken (UPE) 4,50; 2. D. Smit (US) 3,90; 3. R. Marcom (VSA) 3,75.
DG: 1. D. V. Visser (Bell) 46,52; 2. J. Coetzee (US) 43,98; 3. A. Barnard (ST) 43,56.
HG: 1. A. Barnard (ST) 70,48; 2. L. de Lange (US) 48,80; 3. W. Pienaar (US) 46,92.
GS: 1. De V. Visser (Bell) 13,67; W. J. Pauw (US) 13,63; 3. N. Venter (Richmond) 13,35.

SEUNS o.19

100: V. Edgar (Vredenburg) 11,0; 2. G. Prinsloo (Winshoek) 11,3; 3. H. Katzen (CH) 11,6.
200: 1. V. Edgar (V) 22,7; 2. F. Erasmus (Paarl) 22,8; 3. G. Prinsloo (SWA) 23,0.
800: 1. G. Nieuwoudt (US) 1:56,7; 2. W. Trautman (Wel) 1:57,1; 3. L. Erasmus (US) 1:57,8.
2 000: 1. E. Green (PE) 5:29,5; 2. J. Dreyer (Paarl) 5:30,0; 3. B. Engelbrecht (DU) 5:45,8.
1 500 (o.15): 1. J. Lambrechts (Durbanville) 4:15,3; 2. R. Prins (Paarl) 4:24,0; 3. A. Smuts (UGM) 4:26,6.

VETERANE

200: 1. R. Austin (Australië) 22,1); 2. J. Rabie (Wanderers) 22,9; 3. A. Newton (VSA) 24,0; 4. V. Parish (VSA) 24,2.
400 (70—74 jaar): 1. H. Chapson (Hawaii) 70,6; 2. L. Gregory (VSA) 75,6; H. Andrews (CH) 83,0.
800: 1. J. Howes (UK) 2:05,1; 2. B. Heyneman (CH) 2:10,4; 3. J. Theron (US) 2:14,7.
3 000: 1. A. Conradie (W) 9:10,2); 2. P. O'Brien (CH) 9:30,8; 3. A. Richards (VSA) 10:36,2.
1 500: 1. A. Conradie (W) 4:23,7; 2. P. O'Brien (CH) 4:27,0; 3. L. Benning (CH) 4:44,5.
VS: 1. M. Andrews (VSA) 6,13; 2. M. Jackson (VSA) 6,11; 3. M. Newton (VSA) 5,78.

VROUE

100: 1. M. Meyer (W) 12,3; 2. C. Verster (Tyg) 12,4; 3. R. Swart (George) 12,4.
200: 1. R. Swart (George) 25,6; 2. M. Meyer (W) 25,7; 3. B. Swart (W) 26,4.
400: 1. E. du Toit (US) 57,0; 2. L. Verster (Tyg) 58,0; 3. H. Rust (Bell) 59,3.
800: 1. R. Sedibane (Pret) 2:12,0; 2. H. Steyn (Sasol) 2:12,9; 3. M. Nel (Tyg) 2:20,6.
110 H: 1. A. Bezuidenhout (Tyg) 15,2; 2. M. Meyer (W) 17,0.
VS: 1. M. Meyer (W) (5 m 94); 2. M. Berowsky (Pîne) 5,78; 3. I. Essterhuizen (Tyg) (5 m 32).
DG: 1. T. Swanepoel (US) 35,66; 2. R. Theron (Kempt) 35,56; 3. D. van Reenen (US) 34,16.
SG: 1. T. Swanepoel (US) 43,06 m; 2. D. van Zyl (Paarl) 27,92; 3. A. Truter (Bell) 26,52.
GS: 1. T. Swanepoel (US) 12,17; 2. I. van Reenen (US) 11,52; 3. H. Kotze (Piketberg) 11,46.

MEISIES o.18

100: 1. R. Swart (George) 12,6; 2. H. Rust (Strand) 12,8; 3. B. Swart (Windhoek) 12,8.
1 500: 1. P. Sharples (CH) 4:39,4 (W.P.-rekord); 2. R. Sedibane (Pret) 4:41,5; 3. N. Matthee (DU) 4:49,9.
100 H: 1. E. Esterhuizen (Tyg) 15,9; 2. M. du Toit (Robertson) 16,1.

ROSE SEDIBANE van Pretoria staan hier met die trofee wat sy ontvang het as wenner van die 800 m vir vroue gister in die Paarl. Heloïse Steyn (regs) van Sasolburg was tweede en die Matie Marieta Nel (links) derde.

Clip from Die Burger, 28 December 1976, showing Rosina receiving her trophy for the 800m at the Paarl Boxing Day games

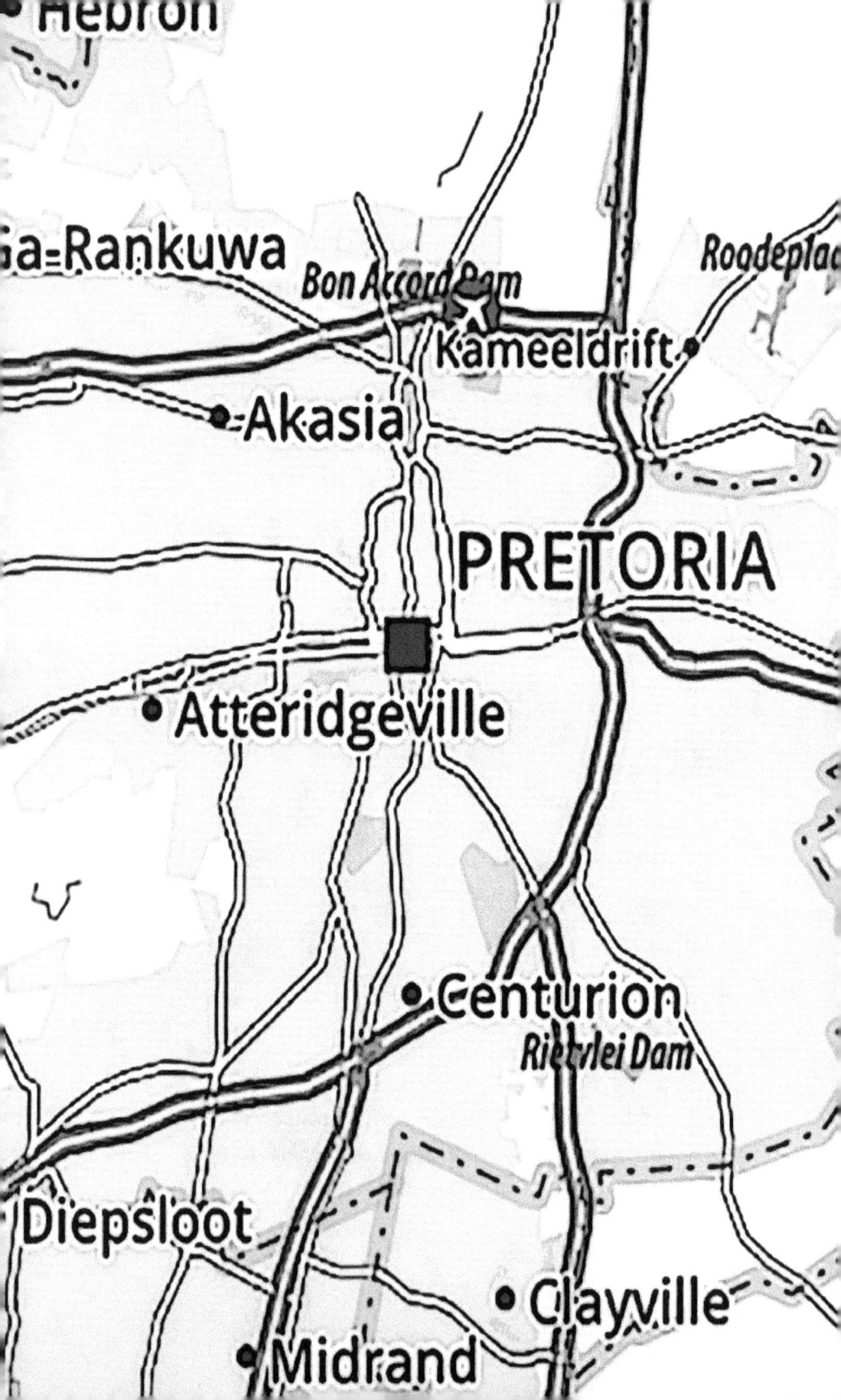

Hebron

Ga-Rankuwa

Bon Accord Dam

Roodeplaa

Kameeldrift

Akasia

PRETORIA

Atteridgeville

Centurion

Rietvlei Dam

Diepsloot

Clayville

Midrand

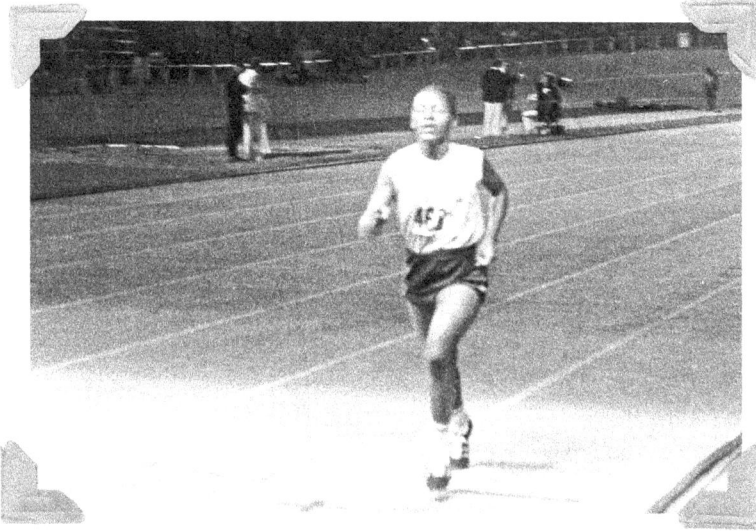

Margaret Sedibane in the 3 000m, in which
she came third after her sister Rosina's
second place at the RAU Championship

CHAPTER 7

Racing for glory

Today, Pretoria is still South Africa's
capital and the seat of government. It
was here, in the Union Buildings, that
the apartheid government crafted its
segregationist policies.

Under the apartheid laws, many places were designated as "white-only" areas, where access for black people was heavily restricted.

Many of the stadiums were situated in designated white areas, where black athletes were only able to participate if they were invited by white sports administrators. Rosina's parents and family members were often unable to support her as they were not allowed into these areas. John Malapane, the celebrated Sepedi commentator for Radio Lebowa, became the voice of the people of Atteridgeville who could not travel to see Rosina's historic races.

> For black South Africans, Rosina's victories were about far more than the athletics. They were about dignifying black lives amid the brutality of apartheid.

From Atteridgeville to Temba, the townships of Pretoria were profoundly proud of Rosina. Even though the number of black people at the stadium was limited, their applause each time Rosina won made up for it. On the occasions when Rosina's siblings, Margaret and Zachariah, were allowed to watch her from the stadium, Zachariah remembers the thunderous cheers and ululating in support of Rosina.

Dr Mary Tsebe, then an eighteen-year-old resident of Atteridgeville, remembers the mood: "We were so proud of her. Everyone in Atteridgeville knew Rosina Sedibane. We used to sit in large groups in front of the radio whenever she was running, and we would scream whenever the radio commentator announced with this distinctive voice that Rosina had won a race."

SPRINGBOK Sonja Laxton who will be making her third appearance in a meeting in Port Elizabeth this season in an attempt to improve the South African 1,500 metres record. Her record is 4:13,1.

Sonja Laxton, pictured here in The Herald newspaper before winning first place in the 800m at the RAU Championship, 1977

For black South Africans, Rosina's victories were about far more than the athletics. They were about dignifying black lives amid the brutality of apartheid.

◇◇◇

It was against this politically fraught background that Rosina began another stellar year of running. In March 1977, during the Black Championships held at Western Holdings mine in Welkom, Rosina ran two different races two days in succession, winning the 1 500 metres on 19 March and the 800 metres the next day. She made history yet again as the first black female athlete to compete at the Pilditch Stadium, and the first to win a provincial title in the multiracial races by beating crowd favourite Ria Hugo in the 1 500 metres.

Later that year, Rosina and her sister Margaret competed against each other in the multiracial championships at the Rand Afrikaans University (RAU, now the University of Johannesburg). There, Sonja Laxton took first place in the 800 metres and Rosina came third. Rosina came second in the 3 000 metres, with Margaret behind her in third position in the same race.

Paarl Boxing Day games, 1977 — the second
picture below shows Rosina coming in second

In the same year, she competed in four other meets, repeating her winning streak at the 1977 annual Paarl Boxing Day games when she won the 1 500-metre race and coming second in the 400- and 800-metre races.

◇◇◇

Rosina's parents had encouraged all their children to be independent at a young age. Two of their three daughters were now professional athletes. Their son, Zachariah, was a sprinter in Coach Mokoka's acclaimed Atteridgeville Athletics Club before he turned to his first love, soccer. They had always emphasised the value of education and the consequences that come with one's choices – lessons that had stood their disciplined children in good stead.

Rosina's parents had encouraged all their children to be independent at a young age.

It was those same proud parents that were deemed less than human by having to carry a **dompas** at all times to be allowed in "white spaces". It was those same parents who had to use a separate entrance reserved for black people when they came to watch their brilliant daughters.

Johannes Sedibane, that same proud father, went to town without fail to engrave Rosina's trophies after her every win. Johannes worked at the Voortrekker Hoogte, an apartheid-era military base, where he proudly showed off his daughter's trophies. The engraver he used was none other than the father of Ria Hugo, Rosina's competitor. After Rosina won against Ria, Mr Hugo refused to engrave Rosina's trophies again.

Sydney and Rosina with Olympian John Carlos during his visit to South Africa in 1976

CHAPTER 8

A dream cut short

Rosina was a force in athletics in the country, dominating in both the black federation and the multiracial meets. In 1977 she became the first woman to break three national records in the same year.

In February 1978, Rosina met Sonja Laxton again at the Ford Invitational in Port Elizabeth. As had happened the year before, Sonja Laxton denied Rosina first position and Rosina came in third. The next month, Rosina was due to travel to South West Africa (now Namibia) to compete in the 400- and 800-metre races. At the time, South African apartheid laws were extended to South West Africa and denied political rights to black citizens. Rosina and her team were prevented from boarding a commercial flight to South West Africa, and were instead forced to cram into a military cargo plane.

Rosina's success was now a regular occurrence in the local athletic community. The sight of her competitors trailing behind her was becoming a frequent event – there seemed to be no real competition for her.

Despite these taxing circumstances, Rosina beat all the other girls for first position in the 800 metres, and was placed second in the 400 metres.

In April 1978, two months after winning the 800 metres at the Western Holdings Maze Black championships in Welkom, Rosina stormed to glory once more at the SASAU Championships in Amanzimtoti, in both the 800- and 1 500-metre races. Rosina's success was now a regular occurrence in the local athletic community. The sight of her competitors trailing behind her was becoming a frequent event – there seemed to be no real competition for her.

◇◇◇

Coach Mokoka recalls that after the 1976 uprisings, black people became more emboldened to challenge the status quo. With the international community watching, the apartheid government and its police had to be cautious not to evoke a backlash.

Tommie Smith and John Carlos are two African American Olympians who visited South Africa to support black athletes during this time. During the 1968 Olympics in Mexico, where they had won gold and bronze respectively in the 200-metre sprint, the two star athletes had raised their fists during the medal ceremony in protest against racial injustice and poverty in the United States. That moment has become one of the most iconic sporting images of the twentieth century.

Life was about to present her with a major setback.

Even though they were expelled from the Olympic village and ostracised by their country for their political stance, Smith and Carlos continued to speak out and stand up for global racial justice. In 1976 they came to South Africa to run sports clinics in the townships and to motivate athletes to get scholarships for American universities.

Rosina and Sydney Maree were two of the athletes that came onto their radar. Within a few years, Sydney would make the trip abroad. But although Coach Mokoka made arrangements for Rosina to join him, life was about to present her with a major setback.

◇◇◇

In 1997, Rosina reflected to Sipho Mthembu of the *Sowetan* about a mysterious injury: "I was busy with my domestic chores at home, moving between the stove and the kitchen table, when I slipped and suffered excruciating pain in my right knee. I went to reputable doctors but they could not diagnose a thing."

Rosina remembers thinking it was a minor injury, which her sisters, Margaret and Grace, treated with ice. The next day, she spent twelve hours at Kalafong Hospital, with doctors unable to explain the injury. X-rays didn't show anything amiss. Splints were put in her leg for two weeks and a plaster of Paris cast was set for six weeks. It was only after the cast was removed that doctors diagnosed her with lateral meniscus – Rosina had cracked her cartilage.

Rosina's injury made newspaper headlines but the medics assured her that she would be able to run

Even though they were expelled from the Olympic village and ostracised by their country for their political stance, Smith and Carlos continued to speak out and stand up for global racial justice.

again. In January 1979, during an interview with Gabu Tugwana of the *Rand Daily Mail*, Coach Mokoka said: "I have been assured by her doctors that Rosina will surely go back to athletics without trouble. Tell all the girls and boys who have been inspired by her that they should not worry. I'll give it a week then we will be starting to give her leg special treatment."

> "I had steeled myself against all odds, but the injury was the final blow and brought down the curtain on my career," she told the *Sowetan* two decades later.

Coach Mokoka organised physiotherapy for Rosina and she tried going back to the track. She recalls being so desperate to resume her running that she ended up subjecting her leg to all sorts of "quick fix" treatments, but in the end she could no longer work out as much as she needed to.

At the time of her injury, she had been at the pinnacle of her career.

"I had steeled myself against all odds, but the injury was the final blow and brought down the curtain on my career," she told the *Sowetan* two decades later.

The pain of her ill-fated loss was so deep that afterwards she completely avoided watching her peers run.

Above and left: Inter-house races at Mamokgalake Chuene College of Education in Lebowa (now Limpopo), 1986

CHAPTER 9

A love story

Rosina's three grown-up daughters, Sue-Ann, Angele and Jo-Anne, remember the day their father, Elisha, called them to the dining-room table to tell them the story of how he met their mother.

> Elisha and Rosina
> went to the same high
> school, Hofmeyr High in
> Atteridgeville, and they
> knew each other from
> there and from church.

Elisha was born to a strict father and stay-at-home mother, and he grew up in Atteridgeville. Unlike Rosina, who came from a large family, Elisha had only one sibling, an older sister. Elisha and Rosina went to the same high school, Hofmeyr High in Atteridgeville, and they knew each other from there and from church. In 1976, seventeen-year-old Rosina was in Form 3 and nineteen-year-old Elisha was a high school senior. They went out together several times but did not consider themselves a couple, at least as far as Rosina was concerned.

One morning at school, Rosina was called to the principal's office. She was already a local household name in athletics by then, so she assumed the meeting was about that. When she arrived, she was surprised to find a panel of official-looking people waiting for her, and soon she was being bombarded with questions about a boy named Elisha Modiba. The people wanted to know how she knew him.

"I told them I did not know any Elisha, and I was dead serious," she recalls. But she later learnt that Elisha was the boy she and everyone else knew as Oupa.

Elisha had been walking back home one evening after seeing Rosina when a gang had attacked him, accusing him of disrespecting them by dating a girl from their part of Atteridgeville. They wanted to claim the famous Rosina for themselves.

"The rest, as they say, is history," says Rosina. "Like all teenagers, I was flattered by the attention and right then Oupa, known as Elisha, and I officially became a couple."

The two youngsters lived a distance from each other, but Elisha would walk back and forth four kilometres every day to visit Rosina. He later joined Coach James Mokoka's Atteridgeville Athletics Club as a runner and even competed in the inter-high championships – but confessed to Rosina that he'd only joined to be closer to her.

◈◈◈

By 1979, the year Rosina entered her senior year, Elisha had matriculated and become a teacher at their same high school. Rosina and Elisha were in a precarious situation: the school had strict rules against teachers entering into romantic relationships with students. The young couple had to appear before the school authorities, but an exception was made in their case because it was an open secret in Atteridgeville that they had been in a relationship before Elisha became a teacher. Rosina's parents only learnt of the relationship the following year, when the Modiba delegation came to their home to pay **lobola** for the 21-year-old Rosina.

> Rosina and Elisha were in a precarious situation: the school had strict rules against teachers entering into romantic relationships with students.

After she finished high school, Rosina and Elisha were married, and Rosina began her studies to become a teacher. Their first daughter, Sue-Ann Modiba, was born in 1982. Rosina stayed home to look after her baby, and then returned to college in 1984. Elisha was a supportive husband committed to being the baby's primary caregiver during this time – a view that did not sit well with his parents and some members of the community.

Elisha's maternal grandfather was a pastor in the Lutheran Church and was a big influence in his life. For a time he had wanted to follow in his footsteps, but Rosina would hear none of it: she did not want to be a pastor's wife. Elisha's second love was music, and he decided to follow his passion, studying via correspondence through the Royal School of Music. He obtained all his courses *cum laude*, which paved the way for him to study further at the University of Zululand for four years, aided by the piano Rosina had bought for his twenty-sixth birthday.

Elisha was a supportive husband committed to being the baby's primary caregiver during this time – a view that did not sit well with his parents and some members of the community.

Rosina receives a trophy
at Mamokgalake Chuene
College, 1986

◈◈◈

Despite her injury, Rosina's running bug had not left her. As a teaching student, she went on to become the college champion in the 800- and 1 500-metre races. In 1985 she won the SA inter-colleges (black) 800 metres. Rosina's last competition was the inter-colleges at Kings Park (now Moses Mabhida Stadium) in Durban in 1986. Rosina stopped running competitively after this, but continued to participate in fun-runs to keep in shape.

> Despite her injury, Rosina's running bug had not left her.

In 1987, Rosina started teaching at Mangena-Mokone Primary School in Atteridgeville, where she would stay for the next decade. She became an athletics coach at the school and, like her former coach James Mokoka, focused on female athletes.

In 1987, Rosina started teaching at Mangena-Mokone Primary School in Atteridgeville, where she would stay for the next decade. She became an athletics coach at the school and, like her former coach James Mokoka, focused on female athletes.

But Rosina lamented the fact that black schools, unlike their white counterparts, did not offer athletics as a year-round sport, a sentiment shared by her former coach. She pointed out that when the township schools championships ended after the three-month track season, nothing happened. She also realised that there was a lack of consistency

It pained Rosina to see that the gender bias she had managed to overcome was still a factor in school sports.

in sports, especially in athletics at school level. Although Mangena-Mokone's athletics team was performing exceptionally well, children fell off the radar when they left for high school.

She later told Sipho Mthembu of the *Sowetan*: "I had assembled a formidable team at Mangena-Mokone. My emphasis was on female athletics. My dream has been to approach as many as I could. My heart, however, bleeds when they go to high school and forget about athletics. They feel they have outgrown the sport. There is one girl I identified … She had everything to be one of the best sprinters in the country. I almost cried when I saw her watching from the stands. She is obviously a big girl now and cannot run."

It pained Rosina to see that the gender bias she had managed to overcome was still a factor in school sports.

Elisha at the piano, a birthday present from Rosina, while little Sue-Ann enjoys the music

Family life

Rosina and Elisha's second daughter, Angele, was born in March 1990. Rosina and Elisha grew their family in a spirit of deep love and mutual trust.

Rosina says Elisha was an unusual African man for his generation. He changed his daughters' diapers, took them to clinics for their immunisations and encouraged his wife to pursue her dreams. Throughout their married life, he called Rosina "The Girl" as a term of endearment.

> Rosina says Elisha was an unusual African man for his generation.

Education meant everything to the couple, and both worked hard towards their goals. Elisha obtained a Fulbright Scholarship in 1992 to study for an MA in Music at Michigan State University in America. He graduated *cum laude* in 1994, while Rosina went on to further her studies at Vista University.

As the couple reached

Elisha competes in athletics — but only to get Rosina's attention!

A party to celebrate Elisha and Rosina's degrees, 1995. Elisha received his master's degree in Music from Michigan State University, USA, in 1994, and Rosina received her BA from Vista University, Pretoria, in 1995.

Doting father Elisha and eldest daughter Sue-Ann holding her baby sister, Jo-Anne, while six-year-old Angele smiles at the camera — taken at Jo-Anne's christening

When Elisha was asked if he was sad that he did not have a son, he got angry and said he'd never wanted one. Instead, he taught his daughters how to change light bulbs and car tyres. He encouraged them to be financially independent and to value education.

for their goals, the country was changing too. After Nelson Mandela's release from prison in 1990, and the first democratic elections of 1994, South Africa was finally free from the clutches of apartheid.

Rosina and Elisha's youngest daughter, Jo-Anne, was born into this "new" South Africa in 1996.

Elisha was a doting father who wanted a good education for his children. The girls didn't have dolls as toys like the other little girls in the township. Instead, Elisha bought them toy cars and books for their birthdays. Angele and Jo-Anne felt their parents never treated them less as girl children. When Elisha was asked if he was sad that he did not have a son, he got angry and said he'd never wanted one. Instead, he taught his daughters how to change light bulbs and car tyres. He encouraged them to be financially independent and to value education.

He started his own home library, and stocked it with children's books and educational toys. Sue-Ann reflects that she was the only one in her class whose comprehension tests and reports were longer than was required – which she puts down to their exposure to literature from a young age at home. Elisha loved his children dearly and told anyone who cared to listen about how wonderful his daughters were. He was family oriented and would go to great extents to help people in need. Known as a disciplinarian, he was overprotective of his children, and never ceased thanking Rosina for looking after them while he was away studying.

When Sue-Ann was a final-year college student, she fell pregnant at the age of twenty. Her parents were disappointed, but as strict and firm as Elisha was, he soon accepted the pregnancy. When Basetsana was born in 2002, no one was prouder than her grandfather: she became the apple of his eye.

ROSINA SEDIBANE MODIBA

SPORT   SCHOOL

AD ASTRA

Rosina Sedibane Modiba Sport School

CHAPTER 11

Rosina Sedibane Modiba Sport School

In early 2000, a former college of education in Pretoria was turned into a sports school for underprivileged but talented children.

It needed a new name, and the Gauteng Legislature called for a submission of the names of outstanding South African women. Many names, including that of a well-known and world-famous South African singer, were put forward. Among them was that of Rosina Sedibane Modiba.

> **As a tribute to her achievements, Rosina's name was selected from the shortlist for the naming of the new school.**

Mike Moloto, a former athlete in the 1970s and an official at the Gauteng Department of Education, thought Rosina would be a perfect fit. It took him months to track Rosina down to ask her for the supporting documents that were required for his submission. Meantime, a City of Tshwane official contacted Rosina's former coach, James Mokoka, asking him for a name of a sportsperson he thought was deserving of the honour. Mokoka also suggested Rosina. One more person suggested Rosina's name and supported this with a presentation on her athletic achievements in the 1970s.

As a tribute to her achievements, Rosina's name was selected from the shortlist for the naming of the new school.

When Mike phoned late one afternoon to tell her that the school would be named after her, Rosina was home with her children. As a music lecturer at a teacher's college in the Free State, Elisha was not there to share in the celebrations, but Rosina remembers the screaming and ululation that engulfed the living room all evening.

Rosina remembers the screaming and ululation that engulfed the living room all evening.

On a Monday morning soon afterwards, the Gauteng Legislature sent an invitation to Rosina's workplace. She was invited to attend a special sitting of the Legislature the very next day as a guest of then Gauteng **MEC** of Education, Mr Ignatius Jacobs. Rosina had no time to prepare, and was not even sure why she had been invited. She asked her school's deputy principal to accompany her to the MEC's office.

> That day – 5 June 2001
> – will remain etched in
> Rosina's mind forever. The
> former Laudium Technical
> College, now one of the
> four elite top sports
> schools in Gauteng, was
> officially renamed the
> Rosina Sedibane Modiba
> Sport School of Focused
> Learning.

The next day, wearing a red-and-black two-piece suit, the 43-year-old mother of three accompanied MEC Ignatius Jacobs to the Legislature, a place in which she had never dreamt she would set foot. When she was introduced in the house as a special guest on that day, she was pleasantly surprised to learn that the event had been convened especially to announce the renaming of the school.

That day – 5 June 2001 – will remain etched in Rosina's mind forever. The former Laudium Technical College, now one of the four elite top sports schools in Gauteng, was officially renamed the Rosina Sedibane Modiba Sport School of Focused Learning. At the sitting, MEC Jacobs described Rosina as a living legend and an unsung hero.

Rosina Sedibane Modiba Sport School is the first sport academy in the country catering solely for talented children who cannot afford the high fees at top sport schools. It is fitting that the school is in Laudium, Rosina's birthplace and the area from which her family was forcefully removed under apartheid.

Although it could never take away the trauma inflicted upon her family and the millions of black people forcefully moved from their ancestral lands, for Rosina and her family the school's renaming was a symbolic effort to redress the injustices of the past.

The Andrew Mlangeni Green Jacket emblem

CHAPTER 12

The Green Jacket

Throughout her running career, Rosina Modiba had defied the lack of proper facilities and a political situation that was stacked against her.

> # Painfully, although she was rated at the top of many athletics events, the administration had denied her the honour of receiving national colours.

For all her athletic ability, as a black woman during apartheid she had still experienced tremendous racial discrimination. Painfully, although she was rated at the top of many athletics events, the administration had denied her the honour of receiving national colours.

Springbok colours was the exclusive domain of white sportsmen and women: participating in an athletics events where Springbok colours were awarded was completely out of the question for black athletes. It would have been an embarrassment for the apartheid government if black athletes were to beat their white counterparts – after all, apartheid was built on the notion that black people were inferior to white people in every way.

◊◊◊

In 2012, more than thirty years after the injury that had tragically ended Rosina's catapultic rise in athletics, Elisha wrote a profile of her many sporting achievements during such a difficult time in the country's history. The letter motivated for the new democratic government's Ministry of Sport to celebrate Rosina by awarding her the sporting colours that had eluded her. After that, Elisha kept a close eye on the sport bulletins in the media in the hope that he would find an announcement regarding his wife.

Poignantly, Elisha had promised Rosina that he would always be with her, even in death. A month after his funeral, Rosina was contacted by the Ministry of Sport to inform her of the intention to honour her with an Andrew Mlangeni Green Jacket.

In October 2013, Elisha lost his battle with diabetes. Rosina, their three daughters and their granddaughter were devastated by his passing. Poignantly, he had promised Rosina that he would always be with her, even in death. A month after his funeral, Rosina was contacted by the Ministry of Sport to inform her of the intention to honour her with an Andrew Mlangeni Green Jacket, alongside seven inductees from different sporting codes.

Named in honour of Rivonia trialist and struggle stalwart Andrew Mlangeni, who was imprisoned on Robben Island alongside Nelson Mandela, the jacket is awarded to unsung sporting heroes from the apartheid era – those talented sportspeople who contributed tirelessly and yet have been denied opportunities and recognition.

Rosina cites receiving the Andrew Mlangeni Green Jacket as the highlight of her sporting life. Besides her family, no one was prouder of this achievement than her school community. The morning after Rosina was awarded her green jacket, learners from Bathokwa lined up the streets of Atteridgeville to welcome their hero. Rosina was hoisted above the crowd as children and teachers celebrated this historic achievement. The Atteridgeville community joined in on the celebrations, which lasted a whole morning.

The Bathokwa Primary School Badge

CHAPTER 13

A new dawn

Rosina spent over three decades
as a teacher.

Before her retirement in 2019, she was the Foundation Phase head of department at Bathokwa Primary School in Saulsville, a township just outside Atteridgeville – the same school Chrystal Nkwana was principal of when she first heard Rosina Sedibane Modiba's name.

> The athletic bug is never far away from Rosina's life. She was a sports coordinator at the school, and worked with a few outstanding girl athletes towards success in athletics. Now that she has more free time, she's become an avid hiker.

The athletic bug is never far away from Rosina's life. She was a sports coordinator at the school, and worked with a few outstanding girl athletes towards success in athletics. Now that she has more free time, she's become an avid hiker.

Her biggest wish is for the government to invest in coaching clinics for school sports administrators and equipping underprivileged schools with good sports facilities.

Following the naming of the Rosina Sedibane Modiba Sport School, Rosina has received more recognition for her achievements. In 2003, Christ Centred Church in the heart of Rosina's beloved Atteridgeville honoured her with an Outstanding Service Award.

Then the Gauteng Department of Education's Tshwane South District awarded Rosina a Momentous Self-Sacrifice award in 2008/2009. This award recognises outstanding people in the community who have contributed towards the country's freedom at great cost to their personal well-being.

In 2012 Rosina was awarded a Lifetime Achievement Award by the Super Shongwe Memorial Charity in association with the local chapter of the Callies Social Gold Club.

In 2014 she was a recipient of the glamorous Women in Sport award by the Department of Sport and Recreation under then Sports Minister Fikile Mbalula.

The Gauteng School Sport Awards in association with the Gauteng Department of Sport, Arts, Culture and Recreation gave her a Special Award in recognition of her outstanding contribution to the development of school sport in 2015.

The following year, former Gauteng Sport MEC Ms Faith Mazibuko awarded Rosina a Lifetime Achievement award and former Minister of Sport Thulas Nxesi awarded her the Ministerial Recognition Award in association with Gsport, an online initiative launched to raise the profile of South African women in sport.

In 2013 the Gauteng Department of Sports and Recreation initiated an exhibition celebrating forgotten heroes of colour in South African Sport prior to democracy. In March 2018 the exhibition travelled to Freedom Park in the City of Tshwane, where a wall for each of these heroes was unveiled. Rosina was one of the heroes.

To this day, the country's athletics body, Athletics South Africa, has never acknowledged Rosina.

Epilogue

Today, Coach James Mokoka's wish is for the government to tap into the experience of former athletes like Rosina to train young people in the townships and rural heartlands. His biggest concern is the lack of sport in schools in the townships, as this is the place to grow South Africa's next crop of athletes to compete in the highest echelons of the athletic world. James also laments the lack of consistency in athletics coaching. He cites retired American sprinter and four-time Olympic gold medalist Michael Johnson as the epitome of coaching success – Johnson stayed with his coach for over twenty years.

Today, Coach James Mokoka's wish is for the government to tap into the experience of former athletes like Rosina to train young people in the townships and rural heartlands.

Mokoka says that black coaches, especially those working in townships, are still not faring better in the new South Africa. They lack resources and the facilities to train their athletes to be competitive. These days, he says, once athletes have attained fame, they leave the township coaches who started with them for better-equipped suburban coaches who have access to a more advanced world of sport. What he would like most is to teach young black athletes financial literacy and motivate them to prioritise education. He has seen many promising athletes unable to realise their dreams after injuries, with nothing to fall back on due to the lack of a formal education.

Mokoka says that black coaches, especially those working in townships, are still not faring better in the new South Africa.

◈◈◈

The history books exclude or underplay the role that women play in society, especially black and brown women. Young people of colour are not frequently exposed to reading material that addresses the challenges they face or that celebrates the achievements of ordinary people from their communities. Rosina not only faced racial discrimination at the height of apartheid, she also overcame the hardships of growing up poor in a society that did not celebrate her choice of becoming an athlete. Despite that, as a young black girl, she became one of the most decorated athletes of her time, and a role model to many.

The history books exclude or underplay the role that women play in society, especially black and brown women.

Rosina Sedibane Modiba's historic 1975 win against a whites-only subsidised South African Athletics Federation remains unknown to many South Africans. She has received little recognition in the new dispensation for her contribution to South African society by breaking racial barriers.

South Africa has so many unsung heroes and heroines from townships, small towns and rural areas, whose stories are never told. Rosina's biography is a celebration of such people and the communities from which they come.

Sources

Brink, Elsabe and Malungane, Gandhi, *Soweto, 16 June 1976: Personal Accounts of the Uprising*, Kwela Books, 2006

Gauteng Department of Sport, Arts and Culture and Recreation: https://provincialgovernment. co.za/units/view/42/gauteng/sport-arts-culture-and-recreation

Kooma, Siza, *Sowetan*, March 16, 1989

Mthembu, Sipho, *Sowetan Sport*, May 22, 1997

Steyn, Dewald, *History of the South African Cross-Country, Middle Distance Running and Walking 1894 to 2014*, Volume 3 – 1975 to 1987

Tugwana, Gabu, *Supplement to the Rand Daily Mail*, January 31, 1979

About the author

Lorato Trok was born and raised in the small Northern Cape town of Kuruman. She is a published author of numerous children's books in Setswana and English, and has facilitated creative writing workshops in South Africa, Swaziland, Zambia, Lesotho and Kenya.

In 2017 she was one of the Association of Non-Fiction and Academic Authors of South Africa (ANFASA) writing grant recipients.

This is her first biography for young people, the first in her series of unsung heroes and heroines in the townships and rural heartlands of South Africa.

Glossary

apartheid: A system of oppression against black people, and classified by the United Nations as a crime against humanity

Bantustan: A homeland for black people set up by the apartheid government to keep different races separate

diketo: A traditional game whereby two players dig a small hole and each try to throw ten small stones into it. The first person to throw all of their stones into the hole is the winner.

dompas: The "dompas" came into existence with the Natives Act of 1952 or the "Pass Law" as it was known. The act made it compulsory for black South Africans over the age of sixteen to carry a "pass book" whenever they were in areas declared as "white areas" (where white people lived).

Group Areas Act: The Group Areas Act of 1950 was legislation enacted by the apartheid government limiting property rights of Indian, coloured and African people.

lobola: The Southern African cultural practice of paying a bride price

MEC: Member of the Executive Council

morabaraba: A chess-like game played with stones in black communities

mosadi: A Setswana word for "woman"

mosetsana: A Setswana word for "girl"

Northern Transvaal: Until 1994, South Africa had only four provinces. The Transvaal included what is now Gauteng, the North West, Limpopo and Mpumalanga. The Northern Transvaal region included Pretoria and Limpopo.

Soweto: South Africa's biggest township and the starting point of the 1976 uprisings

Soweto uprising: A protest that started on 16 June 1976 in response to a decree by the Department of Bantu Education that Afrikaans be used as a language of instruction in secondary schools. After a violent confrontation with police, the uprising claimed at least 176 lives, including of a number of schoolchildren. Among them was Hector Peterson, who was one of the first to be shot. Soweto was the epicentre of the revolt, which soon spread throughout the country.

Springbok colours: The national colours awarded to teams or individuals representing South Africa in international sports competitions

Tshwane: The name for the municipality that includes Pretoria. The City of Tshwane is the second-largest municipality in Gauteng and the administrative capital of South Africa.

,

www.ingramcontent.com/pod-product-compliance
Lightning Source LLC
Chambersburg PA
CBHW071819020426
42331CB00007B/1545